EXPEDITION EVEREST

LEGEND OF THE FORBIDDEN MOUNTAIN

THE JOURNEY BEGINS

Disney
EDITIONS

New York

Across the Himalayas, places are set aside to be used only for meditation and enlightenment. Ancient traditions and practices protect these places.

Legend holds . . . from Nepal to India to China . . . that high in the mountains lives a creature that haunts the remote forests and fiercely guards these lands, long considered sacred . . . and forbidden. Belief in this protector has kept thousands of acres of land pristine. The region around Mount Everest is such a place . . . .

Saisima, Nepal

" . . . You couldn't look at the forests where the yeti is said to live - so extraordinary, so mysterious - without believing that something was there. They seem haunted, ancient, watchful. It is no coincidence that the legend of the yeti withers when the forests are destroyed. The yeti is like the spirit of the forest itself, transcendent, mystical, and strange, something that is more than natural, yet something real that lives and dies as a part of nature."

Tengboche, Nepal

". . . We met with the Rinpoche and asked about the legend of the yeti and the Sherpa people. When the Rinpoche was young, the yeti had come right down to the edge of the monastery. It was during the snowy season, and the yeti just stared into the monastery compound for about half an hour while everyone stared back. The Rinpoche claimed that the yeti has poor eyesight. He said that the yeti is mentioned in ancient Tibetan texts and that it was once commonly reported in the Khumjung, but recent development and traffic had changed that. Few people ever spoke of seeing the yeti these days."

Ding Guo Shan, China

". . . The monks find hairs of the yeti high up in trees where it rubs itself. To indicate how high up, an older monk gestured to an eave line about nine feet above the ground. He described the hair as being streaky blond-brown but mentioned that it appeared bluish when held up to sunlight. The Living Buddha described a recent sighting of the yeti, which appeared at the far edge of the meadow above the monastery in May last year, and again the following June. The young monks, who are children, were afraid, but the older monks took great joy from this. It meant that the forest was pristine. The yeti only appears when the forest is pure and undisturbed."

ABOVE: Yeti image drawn at Tengboche, Nepal. LEFT TO RIGHT: Yeti images drawn at Ding Guo Shan, China. Left and right yeti images were drawn by two monks, while the middle image was drawn by Joe Rohde based on further interviews with them.

DISNEY'S ANIMAL KINGDOM PARK's newest attraction, Expedition Everest, takes guests into the realm of the yeti in the Himalayas, with its amazing landscape and mystical associations. While the ride offers coasterlike thrills as passengers speed through the snowy peaks of the mountain, it also reflects upon the legend of the yeti as a guardian of the environment. The traditional practices of Himalayan people harmonize well with the message of Disney's Animal Kingdom, which is the respect for nature in all of its expressions.

Because of this strong correlation, two expeditions, to China and the Eastern Himalayas, were mounted between August and October 2005.

ABOVE: **Door to gompa in Mustang, Nepal.** BELOW: **The eastern Himalayas near Makalu, site of the journey for Expedition Everest: Mission Himalayas.**

Expedition Everest: Mission Himalayas brought together Imagineers from Disney theme parks; biologists, botanists, and other technical experts from Conservation International's Rapid Assessment Program (RAP); and nonfiction film-makers from renowned Discovery Networks in a scientific inventory of little-known but potentially important conservation sites. The travelers went to areas with a strong yeti oral tradition to research both the legend of the protector yeti itself and to look for undiscovered species of animals and plants.

"Our interests were both cultural and biological," says executive designer and vice president Imagineering Joe Rohde. "We concentrated on areas where the legend of the yeti persists: the Khumbu and Makalu-Barun regions of Nepal, home to Sherpa and Bhotia people, and the Tibetan cultural regions of southwest China. These areas combine the folk traditions of the yeti with areas of great biological value. The yeti's traditional role as 'protector of the sacred' has been integral to preservation in this region. By examining these beliefs, we can learn more about how traditional attitudes encourage conservation behavior. By searching for undiscovered animals and plants under the banner of the ultimate undiscovered creature, we reinforce what the Himalayan people have known for centuries: that all life deserves respect, compassion, and a place in the world."

RIGHT: **Ding Guo Shan Monastery, China.** FAR RIGHT: **Kagbeni Village, Nepal.** BELOW LEFT TO RIGHT: Joe Rohde discusses the legend of the yeti with the lama at Tengboche, Nepal; A young monk films the Rinpoche in Sichaun, China; Uptrail in Makalu, Nepal. BOTTOM: Tent set-up in Saisima, Nepal.

Due to Tibetan tradition, huge areas of land have been protected for centuries by the practice of nonviolence and the belief that these vast forests are the homes of custodial spirits who defend them. The Sacred Lands program run by Conservation International seeks to legally recognize and guard these ancient sites, many considered *beyuls*—a word describing secret and protected places, traditionally protected by the yeti.

Because the Himalayas' difficult landscape has had limited exploration, the region offered real opportunities to discover new species of plants and animals. Members of Mission Himalayas felt it important to believe that new discoveries were still possible in the world of nature, so part of their goal was to raise awareness for this vast reserve of world biodiversity. No one knows what unknown treasures are waiting to be discovered.

To build a mountain, you must start with the Roof of the World—the Himalayas, where Earth's mightiest peaks scrape the heavens. To enter the Himalayas is to enter a world of giants and gods. Consisting of three more or less parallel ranges, including the Great Himalaya range, these majestic mountains start in the forests of northern India, and run along the edge of the Tibetan plateau, which includes northern Pakistan, Nepal, Bhutan, and southwest China, covering 1,500 miles.

In Hindu mythology, here was the home of Shiva, one of the supreme triad and the lord of animals. Also here, in Hindu and Buddhist mythology, was Mount Meru, the center of the earth, inhabited by gods, particularly Kubera, lord of the treasures of the earth and king of the Yakshas (supernatural beings) who watched over the fertility of the land. The Himalayas,

translated from the Sanskrit as "abode of the gods," truly reflect the respect in which they are held. Other names include Chomo Lhari, "Goddess of the Holy Mountain"; Nanda Devi, named after the goddess Nanda; and Makalu for the god Mahakala.

Mount Everest, called Peak XV upon initial identification, was renamed in 1865 by the British after the then Surveyor-General of India, Sir George Everest. It is, to the residents of Nepal, Sagarmatha, the "Summit of Heaven." Everest is the throne of Migyo Lang Zang, the tiger-riding goddess who warns against the overly developed self, the too-much me. Locally it is known as Jomo Lung Ma, "Goddess of the Wind," or Chomolungma, "Mother Goddess of the World." Records suggest that this was the name preferred by Sir George.

"The ice ages left a light touch on the Himalayas, unlike the Rockies and the Alps, which were scraped clean of any life at all by glaciers. Every living thing we see in those mountains has only been living there since the end of the last ice age. Here, in the eastern Himalayas, life has been evolving for millions of years, and that life was imported from two distinct continents - one tropical and one temperate - the ancient wedge of India and the huge mass of old Asia. The extreme depth and isolation of the valleys provides multiple habitats for new forms of life to arise, as does the extreme change in elevation from the low, hot valleys to the icy mountaintops. Each valley, each slope, is like an island, different from the next valley and so isolated by its landscape that it might as well be separated by miles of ocean. This isolation has not only allowed new forms of life to evolve, it has protected ancient forms of life, prehistoric forms of life that have become extinct elsewhere, and allowed them to continue, hidden, here."

OPPOSITE: Everest, Lhotse, and Ama Dablan, Nepal. ABOVE: View of Tengboche, Nepal. LEFT TO RIGHT: Wuxiu, China; Damji, Bhutan; ChomoLhari, Bhutan.

DISNEY DESIGNERS, ARCHITECTS, and creative storytellers visited several areas of Asia near Mount Everest. Thousands of photographs and

hours of video of Tibetan and Nepalese culture, villages, homes, public spaces, architectures, trees, and plants were collected. Team members visited Buddhist temples and shrines, trekked through the foothills on

Tibetan ponies, and spent many hours talking with locals to learn about their beliefs and traditions. The result is the village of Serka Zong, which consists of several buildings, including a hotel, Internet café, and trekking supply store, all reflective of a contemporary Himalayan village where ancient traditions and modern trends combine.

"Imagineers journeyed to Nepal several times," explains Joe Rohde, "immersing themselves in the legends, lore, and heart of the place. The

goal was to create an authentically detailed environment that reflected the culture and traditions of these Himalayan countries explored during our research. Touching the prayer wheels, hearing the tonal spectrum of bells worn by animals, and seeing how the local people applied color to their homes left a deep impression on us. This experience allowed us to approach this project with an insight and authenticity we could only attain by being there."

TOP LEFT TO RIGHT: Shrine in Kathesimbu, Kathmandu; House in Jiaju, outside Danba, China; Senior concept designer Stefan Hellwig in front of gompa in Kagbeni, Nepal. FAR LEFT: Sketch of Jiaju house. LEFT: Stefan Hellwig examines deformation of walls in Marpha, Mustang, Nepal. OPPOSITE PAGE LEFT: Mandir in Kathmandu. RIGHT: Tagong gompa (Lhakang) in Sichuan, China.

" . . . In Patan, one of the ancient cities near Kathmandu, a beautiful mandir rises in Durbar square. It ascends three tiers, though there are mandirs that rise five, seven, even nine tiers. It's a hypnotic tower of compounded images, carvings upon carvings, rows of detail layered over rows of more detail. Some images are barely visible in the shadows of the overhanging eaves. People cluster on the platform base to bask in the sun or retire to the shade."

" . . . Behind the huge monastic center at Tagong, the largest hill is nearly covered in prayer flags set in triangular patterns to ward off evil. There are thousands of them, flickering in the winds that rake the high, mounded hills. There is a gompa at the other end of the town, and beyond that, a huge prayer-flag line is suspended like a bridge over the entire valley."

" . . . The Tagong gompa is a Sakya monastery, painted brick red as all Sakya temples are. Behind the Lhakang is the chorten garden, within high walls that are probably necessary for defense. The entire outer circuit, which pilgrims circumambulate, is lined with prayer wheels and mani walls."

" . . . The early mornings in Ding Guo Shan were so wrapped in fog that filming was impossible. So we rose at leisure, ate, and waited for the wet mist to rise and the pale sunlight to pierce the cloud roof of our mountaintop. After midday, the mist would begin to settle, and as it became heavier, turn to rain. We retreated to our beautiful cozy rooms and unwound until dinner, just as cozy. Thus, the urgency of work was isolated from the quiet times of the day, and all were able to reflect for a while on just how special it was to be there."

LEGENDS OF GIANT "APE MEN" EXIST on most continents, from North America's Sasquatch and the notably smelly Skunk Ape of the Everglades, to the Yowie of Australia, the wild men of Hupeh, the Yeren in China, and the Russian Alma and Kaptar, as well as others from New Zealand, Africa, and Venezuela. Sightings of yeti in the Himalayan region date back to the 14th century, with the first Westerner sighting in 1832. The creature became more well-known in 1921, when Lieutenant-Colonel C. K. Howard Bury observed unidentifiable creatures in the area between Kharta and Lhakpa La. Asking his Tibetan porters about huge footprints left in the snow, he was told they were made by the *me-teh* (abominable) or *meteh-kangmi* (abominable snow man). This translation, reported by a journalist, did not precisely reflect the porters' actual meaning, which was that the abominable aspect

came from the creature's stinky smell. Yeti derives from *yeh-teh*, which translates as "that-there thing" or "rock-thing."

In 1951, Eric Shipton first photographed huge footprints on the southwestern slope of the Menlung Glacier, which suggested a biped at least eight feet tall. Sir Edmund Hillary (Everest's conqueror along with Sherpa Tenzing Norgay) brought back a skullcap in 1960 purportedly made of yeti hide, though it turned out to be goatskin. The first photograph of a possible living yeti was taken by long-distance runner Anthony Wooldridge in 1986.

Three sizes have been sighted, from the five foot tall *me-teh* to the *dzu-teh*, which towers over eight feet, and they may or may not be related. Author Bernard Heuvelmans proposes that the "wild man" of Asia is of the race *Pithecanthropus*, which lived at the end of the Pliocene period in southwest Asia. Other thoughts are that these creatures are the descendants of *Meganthropus* or possibly a giant ape known as *Gigantopithecus blacki*. Zoologist Edward Cronin speculates that *Gigantopithecus* sought sanctuary in the Himalayan valleys during the Pleistocene Age. Recent discoveries of prehistoric hominids in Southeast Asia provide the intriguing possibility that *Gigantopithecus* still survives in these remote reaches.

"The yeti combines several strands of personal interests. As a potential real creature, it invites logical speculation as to how it could exist. You need to mobilize knowledge of comparative anatomy, the adaptation and radiation of species, paleontology, and geography to weave the web of clues between the yeti today and the ancestor it might have descended from a million years ago. You have to understand enough mathematics to deduce the volume of food material a population of yetis would need to exist, and how many yetis would be in that population to make it viable. You need to collate that with the cultural and geographic information about the people who surround the areas where the yeti might exist and decide whether their impact on the environment leaves any real possibility for a yeti.

" . . . Or you could follow the legend itself and learn about ancient Tibetan culture prior to the conversion to Buddhism. Read the myths and oral traditions as they are written down to see how they are structured. If the yeti myth is very similar to others, then perhaps the yeti is only a story, imported from another tradition and re-dressed in Tibetan style."

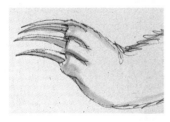

"There is more than one kind of yeti. Each region has its own words for the mysterious hairy creatures of the forest. Some of these types of creatures are easily understood as something we might know - a bear, a hermit. Others are inexplicable. The versions are as numerous as the names: yeti, mehti, dzuti, yeren, mugo, migoi, rakshasa, shokpa, drelmo, ban jhankri, bun manchi, pong rum . . . "

"Eating tiny animals, frogs, and picas is one of the particulars of the yeti. It is said to hunt for picas in high places, thus the footprints in the snow. Another report has the yeti eating the hanging moss, so like Spanish moss, that drapes the trees in the cold high forests of oak and rhododendron. This reminds me of the golden monkeys who eat lichens off the trees in winter."

"I asked the Living Buddha point blank what he thought the yeti was. He replied that it was two things at once. A real animal and an immortal . . . a Chen Yen . . . a deity."

Golden monkeys were observed at the Qinling Mountain preserve near Xian, China with the assistance of primatologists Russ Mittemeier, president of Conservation International, and Dr. Anne Savage from Disney's Animal Kingdom on the Mission Himalayas expedition.

"ONE OF THE MOST IMPORTANT ISSUES confronting the design team," Joe Rohde explains, "was how to imagine a cold-climate primate as big as the yeti. There are very few cold-climate primates in the world, among them the snow monkeys in Japan, which look more or less like the Rhesus monkeys in Kathmandu. The golden monkey, a snub-nosed langur that is much more dramatic looking, is another. They live in isolated populations in the mountains of Sichuan and further north at the edge of Shaanxi Province, in the Qinling Mountains. These were the inspiration for our yeti—strange, haunting faces covered in hair everywhere but in the smallest areas around the unfathomable dark eyes and nose. They have no nasal tissue, which may be an adaptation to the cold winter snows, but it also makes them look spooky. They are a perfect model of a cold-climate primate.

"Almost all the great apes, and also the golden monkey, have large canine teeth, used for display as well as for shredding plant material off their stalks. Anything as big as the yeti has to be primarily herbivorous—there's just not enough meat in the forest for a population of huge carnivores. The prehistoric ape *Gigantopithecus* was most probably a herbivore who, like the giant panda, ate bamboo.

"Our yeti would be a huge, scary version of one of these monkeys," Joe continues, "if it were actually an ape. They have a cape of long hair on their backs like the colobus monkey, and we have incorporated this detail into the myth as well." The pale blue face, especially on the male, is a mark of dominance, and Imagineers incorporated this into the yeti for they wanted it to appear to be a dominant male, as well as using the blueness of the face to suggest cold.

"Size alone is an adaptation to cold," explains Joe. "Big things hold their body heat more efficiently because there is a low ratio of surface area to mass. If the yeti is big, it follows that it is adaptable to cold environments. Some Sherpa, presented with photos of an orangutan, have claimed that this was what a yeti looked like. The prehistoric range of orangutans was much broader than it is today and included areas of

South China, where the legend of the yeti persists. Orangutans are big, and this alone might make them adaptable to a cold environment. Our concept for the yeti is really big, so big that we must imagine our yeti traveling on all fours at times."

Imagineers used the skull of a langur to build the yeti head, but because they were making this animal much bigger than any langur, they needed to adjust its physical features. Additions included more robust cheekbones; a deeper jaw, more like the jaw on the fossil skull of *Gigantopithecus*; and a sagittal crest—a ridge of bone along the top of the skull for attaching huge jaw muscles. "This is one of the weird details in the oral

tradition of the yeti," says Joe with a laugh, "that makes you wonder if there really is, or was, an ape out there. The domed head of the yeti is exactly what you would have in a great ape— jaw muscles that feed up into an extensive sagittal crest. If the people of the Himalayas are just making up the yeti story, how could it be that they have come up with such correct and exact physical details?"

ABOVE: A selection of head, fur, and color studies for the yeti design in Expedition Everest. Computers allowed the artists at Walt Disney Imagineering to experiment with infinite variations.

BELOW LEFT TO RIGHT: Early visual development and color studies based on various species of primates including a combination gibbon/orangutan, a gorilla, and a combination gorilla/langur monkey.

The mammoth-sized Expedition Everest yeti is the most sophisticated Audio-Animatronics figure ever created by Walt Disney Imagineering. Based on the information culled from the Himalayan research, with assistance from Dr. Stuart Sumida, an anatomical consultant to special effects artists and animators, a design was put together after many diverse interpretations were considered.

"Yetis are often described as reddish brown, sort of the color of an orangutan. Sherpas have reportedly pointed to pictures of orangutans as looking to them like the yeti. Only in westernized versions is the yeti white."

"In Nepal, the yeti has long hair that drags behind it when it walks and stirs up the dust in a cloud as it goes through the forest."

"When talking about the yeti at the Ding Guo monastery, they described the hair of the yeti as radiating from its belly . . . that is, that the hair, from the belly up, grows upward and the hair from the belly down grows down. An older monk tried to indicate the stride of the yeti, which seemed to be about five to six feet. They described the feet as long."

"They have a distinctive scream. It's a high, whistling shriek, likened to the call of a large eagle. This detail is identical whether reported in western China or in the Nepalese Himalayas. On the trail in Nepal, this high, keening sound was also described. When asked to imitate it, all the Sherpas cried out 'Aiyeeeeeeeeeeeeeeeeeeeee!' I joined in with them a second time and we all busted up."

THIS PAGE AND OPPOSITE:
Visual development of the yeti by Walt Disney Imagineers.

THE PROCESS OF MAKING A MOUNTAIN begins with sketches, then small paper models that are then sculpted in clay, and finally, foam models. As the concept evolves, the models become more detailed and larger in size. When the final design for Expedition Everest was complete, the six-foot-tall model was scanned into a computer using laser technology. Show programmers and animation designers were able to review a computer model that allowed them to program the thrill ride "virtually" before construction even began. The resulting digital files were then used to create and bend the steel needed for the massive structure, which was close to 200 feet tall when completed.

Although Imagineers blended styles from several regions of the Himalayas to create Serka Zong, the architecture is largely based on the Kali Gandaki region of the Annapurna Conservancy area. Wood elements were designed and built in Nepal by Newari woodcarvers. Artists used hammers, chain saws, and blowtorches to "age" wood and buildings in the village, making them look like longstanding features of the landscape. The design team studied Tibetan and Nepalese building materials, eventually choosing two basic methods of construction: stone buildings such as the dressed stone in the Tea Warehouse and dry-laid stone in the simpler village building; and a technique called "rammed earth," where slightly moistened dirt is placed in a large box frame in four-inch-high layers and pounded with mallets until the layers are packed as hard as concrete. Properly protected, the buildings could last for a thousand years. Over 2,000 hand-crafted items from Asia, including wood, stone, and metal, were used on the architectural orna-mentation, props, and cabinetry. The team also talked with Himalayan monks about earth-based pigments; studied the carved details of local earthen, rock, and wood buildings; and researched cultural iconography—all with the goal of creat-ing an experience that would be so extraordinarily

CLOCKWISE FROM TOP RIGHT: Visual development of train outside mountain; Senior show programmer Rick Daffern (seated) and principal anima-tion designer Larry McAfee review a computer model of Expedition Everest; Scaffolded mountain; Imagineers collabo-rated with Newari carvers, creating the many yeti images seen in the Mandir.

OPPOSITE PAGE TOP: Visual development of upramp into mountainside monastery. MIDDLE RIGHT: (left to right) Frank Newman, Joe Rohde, and Allison Frasier surmount the model phase of making a mountain. MIDDLE LEFT: Visual development of village. BELOW RIGHT: Color model. FAR LEFT AND BOTTOM: Color elevations of buildings in Serka Zong.

immersive and real that visitors might believe, if even for just a moment, they were standing on the other side of the world.

Landscape architects incorporated character-istics from Bhutan, Mustang, Sichuan, and Kath-mandu to capture the diversity of the botanically rich region. More than 900 bamboo plants, inclu-ding 4 species of giant bamboo, 10 species of trees, and 110 species of shrubs were planted to evoke the lowlands surrounding Mount Everest.

Namaste! Tashi delek!

Thank you for choosing Expedition Everest, provided by Himalayan Escapes – Tours and Expeditions, offering unique, guided—and safe!—adventures to the Forbidden Mountain.

When travelers approach the village area that signals the entry to Expedition Everest, they will be transported to the Himalayan region as they walk by colorful flags looping from building to building and pole to pole. Emblazoned with auscpicious symbols, the banners are inspired by the Himalayan prayer flags that send thoughts and prayers into the wind. Along their journey, an ornamental monastery, intricately carved totems, and a garden of stone carvings of the yeti clutching the mountain summon up the rich culture and tradition of this environment.

Before beginning their trek along the lake edge to the village of Serka Zong (Fortress of the Chasm), adventurers will encounter the yeti shrine, mystically aligned with the silhouette of the Forbidden Mountain so that the two mimic each other—the real mountain beyond and the ritual mountain before. Enthroned in the arch is a bronze of the yeti as protector, developed by Newari bronze casters in Kathmandu.

The first building in the village is the Shangri-la Trekkers Inn and Internet Café, representing any number of small village buildings that could be found in the Himalayan foothills. The two-building cluster has a traditional building juxtaposed against the "new" Yeti Palace Hotel, being constructed to take advantage of the expected flow of trekkers who will come to ride the train. A trekker's supply store, Gupta's Gear, is located on the first floor though it's closed, while Gupta is up on the mountain collecting equipment.

Norbu and Bob's is the combination booking and permit offices of Himalayan Escapes. The structure blends Tibetan and Newari influences, with the flat roof and rooftop shrine being part of the highland tradition, and the elaborately carved windows part of the lowland Nepalese tradition. A profusion of electrical wires run along the walls to separate switches for each light and outlet. Each switch has been anointed with dabs of color and images of local gods, in keeping with the reverence for fire as an elemental force. The firewood stored on the roof here and on other buildings is a sign of affluence—firewood is a rare and expensive commodity.

To the right, rolling fields of tea plants slope down to the water. The buildings nearby once supported the harvesting and shipping of tea for the Royal Anandapur Tea Company. The buildings and railroad, abandoned when the company went out of business, due to mysterious circumstances, have been taken over by Himalayan Escapes—Tours and Expeditions and a few local merchants. At the edge of the village is a Tibetan *mani* (prayer) wall.

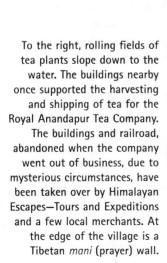

Expedition members then proceed past the Yeti Mandir. The Sanskrit word *mandir* refers to many types of temples and shrines, but implies something big enough to be architecture. This pagoda-type structure is a very ancient form and particularly Nepalese, or more correctly, Newari, and was developed in collaboration with artisans in Kathmandu.

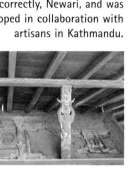

There are one thousand yetis throughout the three-story Mandir. The strut that holds up the deep eaves of the pagoda represents the yeti as the destroyer of yaks. Higher up, the yeti is represented as the defender of the mountain, symbolically reduced to just his hand protectively placed in front of the sacred peak. The small shrine within the Mandir also shows the yeti as protector of the mountain. In this shrine sits a bronze also developed by the Newari bronze casters, showing the yeti in the traditional posture of a defender, holding the three-peaked mountain in one hand and thrusting his other hand out in a "keep back" gesture.

Past the Mandir is Tashi's Trek and Tongba Shop, a local general store selling supplies to expeditions. Inside, it's obvious that Tashi lives right there in the shop. Behind his sleeping cot is a very typical display rack used in Tibetan homes and businesses to show off nice tableware and possessions. This is the general store, the place to pick up last-minute supplies essential for an expedition—oxygen tanks, packs, crampons, gloves, boots, and so forth. There are also a few amenities such as magazines and used paperbacks, and a tongba bar. Tongba is a beverage made by pouring hot water into a pot of fermented millet and is drunk through a bamboo straw.

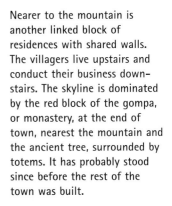

Nearer to the mountain is another linked block of residences with shared walls. The villagers live upstairs and conduct their business downstairs. The skyline is dominated by the red block of the gompa, or monastery, at the end of town, nearest the mountain and the ancient tree, surrounded by totems. It has probably stood since before the rest of the town was built.

The color on the buildings is rich with symbolic meaning. Red at the corners, as well as red or black around windows, is a form of magical protection. The three stripes on rooftop shrines represent the three spirit worlds. The building with the long stripes all the way down, next to the red gompa, represents a rich, old-money family with ties to the monastery. This complex color symbology is used all across the Tibetan world, with many local variants. Since the new train ride into the mountains seems to have awakened the yeti, everyone is on symbolic high alert.

Adjoining the general store is The Yeti Museum, a large plaster-covered stone and wood building with a high ceiling. It once served as a tea warehouse. Display cases and room dividers have been recently installed as a collection of maps, photos, paintings, and artifacts present the legend, lore, and science of the yeti to visitors to the region.

At the exhibit's conclusion, curator Professor Pema Dorje, Ph.D., has posted a warning:

YOU ARE ABOUT TO ENTER THE SACRED DOMAIN OF THE YETI, GUARDIAN AND PROTECTOR OF THE FORBIDDEN MOUNTAIN. THOSE WHO PROCEED WITH RESPECT AND REVERENCE FOR THE SANCTITY OF THE NATURAL ENVIRONMENT AND ITS CREATURES SHOULD HAVE NO FEAR. TO ALL OTHERS
—A WARNING—
YOU RISK THE WRATH OF THE YETI.

Please note: Himalayan Escapes emphasizes that the opinions expressed by the curator of The Yeti Museum do not reflect the views of the owners and operators of your tour.

EXPEDITION EVEREST MEMBERS ASSEMBLE HERE.

Boarding a refurbished tea plantation train in the Anandapur Rail Service, intrepid travelers are destined for the foot of Mount Everest in the Himalayas. The newly re-opened railway cuts days off the arduous journey to base camp at Everest. Please ignore warnings from the villagers about the giant, mysterious creature said to guard the mountain. Himalayan Escapes assures you of a safe and comfortable trip. Relax and enjoy your journey through thick bamboo forests, past thundering waterfalls, and across shimmering glacier fields, climbing higher and higher into the snow-capped peaks.

At the far end of the station, the train passes through a track switch. The track dips slightly then climbs a grade, passing a shrine erected to honor the sacred yeti.

Following an incline flanked by a ceremonial stairway that ascends the mountain at a steep angle, the track passes through a tunnel carved from the rock beneath an ancient fortress. In the darkness above the track, lit by flickering firelight, is a monumental mural. The mural depicts a monstrous hairy creature, wild-eyed and snarling—the yeti, guardian of Forbidden Mountain.

Beyond the fortress, across a deep chasm, stands an imposing mountain summit. The train crosses the chasm on a creaking iron trestle, then circumvents a mountain tunnel. Then, suddenly, it screeches to a halt. Ahead is a broken trestle, its rails bent and twisted.

A high-pitched, keening cry is heard as a Lammergeier vulture rises into view, hovering on a gust of wind. Then there is a rattle and thunk as the brakes are released. The whistle blasts and the train begins to move backward! And as it does, the chilling howl of the yeti can be heard in the distance, echoing off the surrounding mountains.

Re-entering the mountain, the train stops in a large cavern. On the wall, the shadow of another train crossing a trestle can be seen . . . joined by the shadow of the yeti, who rips up the heavy railings and ties. A sound from your train catches the yeti's attention. With a roar, it leaps forward.

Thunder cracks, lightning flashes, and the train descends to the base of the mountain only to spiral upwards to enter it once again. The train races through mountain caverns and icy canyons as passengers head for an inevitable showdown with the mysterious protector of these hidden reaches. Will it be possible to escape the wrath of this legendary creature? Will the yeti succeed in defending his realm of natural beauty— the Forbidden Mountain?

THANK YOU FOR CHOOSING
HIMALAYAN ESCAPES.

If you enjoyed your trip, don't forget to thank your Sherpa!

23

EXPEDITION Everest™ ©DISNEY

For information address Disney Editions, 114 Fifth Avenue, New York, New York 10011-5690.

Editorial Director: Wendy Lefkon
Senior Editor: Jody Revenson
Editorial Assistant: Jessica Ward

Printed in the United States of America.
Library of Congress Cataloging-in-Publication Data on file.
ISBN: 1-4231-0231-2
Limited Edition
Printed on Recycled Paper

Concept and editorial by Jody Revenson
Art direction and cover design by Alex Eiserloh
Interior design by Jennie Putvin

All photographs, original artwork, and text by Joe Rohde used with permission.

With special thanks to Gene Duncan, Andrea Finger, Jennifer Gerstin, Jason Grandt, Stefan Hellwig, Gary Landrum, Jeff Lepinske, Jan O'Connor, Suzy O'Hara, Debbie Nassayan, Diego Parras, Joe Rohde, Jen Rother, Diane Scoglio, David Stern, Muriel Tebid, Jeff Titelius, and Marilyn Waters.

For more information about Conservation International, please visit www.conservation.org.

For more information on Expedition Everest and Mission Himalayas, please visit www.disneyeverest.com.

CREDITS

Unless otherwise noted, all photography, original artwork, and journal text is by Joe Rohde.

COVER: Dan Goozee
PAGE 2: Protector yeti created by Thangka artist Mr. Gyanu.
PAGE 3: Bottom left and right by monks from Ding Guo Shan, China.
PAGE 5: Below left: Russ Mittlemeier; Below middle: Martin Pailthrop.
PAGE 12: Bottom: Scott Goddard.
PAGE 13: Douglas Griffith
PAGE 14: Top and middle: Scott Goddard; Below and Bottom middle: Ron Husband; Bottom left and right: Chris Turner.
PAGE 16: Top: Chris Turner; Middle right: Jess Allen; Middle left: Ray Spencer; Far left: Stefan Hellwig; Bottom: Andrea Bottancino.
PAGE 17: Clockwise from top right: Chris Turner, Byron J. Cohen, Gene Duncan.
PAGE 18: Top: Gene Duncan
PAGE 19: Top left and right: Gene Duncan; Middle: Diego Parras.
PAGE 20: Top right and Middle: Diego Parras; Bottom: Gene Duncan.
PAGE 21: Top: Diego Parras
PAGE 22: Left: Diego Parras; Middle: Jason Grandt; Bottom: Gene Duncan.
PAGE 23: Top: Diego Parras; Left: Jason Grandt.
INSIDE BACK COVER: Gene Duncan